Robo-Advisors and Beyond: Building a Fintech Startup with AI

By Silas Meadowlark

Index

- The Rise of Robo-Advisors
  - Understanding the Robo-Advisor Landscape
  - The Advantages of Robo-Advisors
  - Challenges and Limitations of Robo-Advisors

- Introducing Artificial Intelligence (AI) in Fintech
  - Exploring AI Concepts and Applications
  - AI-Powered Portfolio Management
  - Personalized Wealth Management with AI

- Building a Fintech Startup with AI
  - Defining Your Fintech Startup's Vision
  - Identifying Key AI Capabilities
  - Developing a Robust AI-Powered Platform

- Data-Driven Decision Making
  - Collecting and Organizing Financial Data
  - Leveraging Machine Learning for Insights
  - Predictive Analytics and Investment Strategies

- Achieving Operational Efficiency with AI
  - Automating Mundane Tasks
  - Enhancing Customer Experience
  - Streamlining Back-Office Operations

- Ensuring Regulatory Compliance
  - Understanding Financial Regulations
  - Implementing Ethical AI Practices
  - Maintaining Transparency and Accountability

- Cybersecurity and Data Privacy
  - Protecting Client Information
  - Implementing Robust Security Measures

- Addressing Emerging Cyber Threats

- Scaling your Fintech Startup
  - Attracting and Retaining Talent
  - Fostering a Culture of Innovation
  - Expanding into New Markets

- Navigating the Fintech Ecosystem
  - Collaborating with Traditional Financial Institutions
  - Leveraging Fintech Partnerships
  - Staying Ahead of Industry Trends

- Marketing and Branding in the Fintech Space
  - Crafting a Compelling Brand Identity
  - Effective Digital Marketing Strategies
  - Building a Robust Client Acquisition Pipeline

- Securing Funding and Investments
  - Exploring Funding Options
  - Pitching to Investors
  - Managing Investor Relations

- Adapting to a Changing Regulatory Landscape
  - Monitoring Regulatory Updates
  - Ensuring Compliance with New Rules
  - Advocating for Fintech-Friendly Policies

- Fostering Client Trust and Loyalty
  - Prioritizing Transparency and Communication
  - Providing Exceptional Customer Service
  - Cultivating Long-Term Relationships

- Leveraging Emerging Technologies
  - Exploring Blockchain and Cryptocurrencies
  - Integrating Voice Assistants and Chatbots
  - Harnessing the Power of the Internet of Things

- The Future of Fintech and AI
  - Anticipating Industry Disruptions

- Preparing for Technological Advancements
- Envisioning the Next Generation of Fintech

The Rise of Robo Advisors

Understanding the Robo Advisor Scene

The investment management industry has undergone a remarkable transformation in recent years, with the rise of robo advisors taking center stage. These digital platforms, powered by sophisticated algorithms and advanced data analytics, have shook up the traditional financial advisory model, offering a new and novel approach to wealth management. As technology continues to shape the future of finance, it's important to understand the robo advisor terrain and its implications for the industry.

Robo advisors are essentially automated investment management services that use computer algorithms to allocate and manage client portfolios. These platforms use advanced algorithms to analyze market trends, assess risk profiles, and create personalized investment strategies tailored to each client's unique financial goals and risk tolerance. By automating many of the traditional financial advisory tasks, robo advisors have been able to offer a more accessible and cost effective alternative to traditional wealth management services.

The emergence of robo advisors has been driven by a confluence of factors, including the increasing demand for personalized and transparent investment solutions, the ubiquity of digital technologies, and the growing need for more affordable and accessible financial advice. As the robo advisor situation continues to evolve, it has captured the attention of both individual investors and the broader financial services industry, leading to a proliferation of players in this dynamic market.

The Advantages of Robo Advisors

Robo advisors have gained popularity due to their ability to deliver a range of compelling advantages to investors. One of the primary benefits of these digital platforms is their cost effectiveness. By leveraging automation and technology, robo advisors can offer investment management services at a fraction of the cost of traditional financial advisors, making professional wealth management accessible to a wider audience.

Another key advantage of robo advisors is their scalability and flexibility. These digital platforms can efficiently manage a large number of client accounts, allowing them to serve a diverse client base with varying investment needs. This scalability enables robo advisors to provide personalized investment strategies and portfolio management services to clients, regardless of their account size or investment experience.

Robo advisors also excel in their ability to provide 24/7 access to investment management services. Clients can monitor their portfolios, make adjustments, and access financial planning tools through user friendly mobile apps and online platforms, offering a level of convenience and accessibility that traditional financial advisors often struggle to match.

Moreover, robo advisors are known for their transparency and data driven decision making. By providing detailed information about their investment strategies, fees, and portfolio composition, these digital platforms aim to encourage a sense of trust and empowerment among their clients, who can closely monitor the performance and progress of their investments.

Challenges and Limitations of Robo Advisors

While robo advisors have revolutionized the wealth management industry, they also face several challenges and limitations that must be addressed. One of the primary concerns is the lack of human interaction and personalized advice. While robo advisors can provide personalized portfolio management, they may struggle to fully understand the delicate financial and life circumstances of each individual client, potentially leading to suboptimal investment strategies.

Another limitation of robo advisors is their reliance on algorithms and data driven decision making. While these digital platforms employ sophisticated algorithms to analyze market trends and make investment decisions, they may not be able to fully account for the complexities and unpredictability of the financial markets. This can lead to investment performance that may not harmonize with a client's long term financial goals or risk tolerance.

Additionally, the regulatory situation surrounding robo advisors is still evolving, and these digital platforms may face increasing scrutiny and compliance requirements as the industry matures. Ensuring adherence to financial regulations, maintaining sturdy cybersecurity measures, and addressing potential ethical concerns regarding the use of algorithms in investment management are all critical challenges that robo advisors must navigate.

Finally, the long term viability and sustainability of robo advisors remain uncertain. As the industry continues to evolve, these digital platforms may face increased competition from traditional financial institutions, as well as the potential disruption of emerging technologies, such as artificial intelligence and blockchain. Adapting to these dynamic changes and maintaining a competitive edge will be essential for robo advisors to thrive in the future.

Introducing Artificial Intelligence (AI) in Fintech

Exploring AI Concepts and Applications

In the rapidly evolving world of finance, artificial intelligence (AI) has emerged as a radical force, upsetting traditional practices and paving the way for new and novel solutions. As fintech startups strive to stay ahead of the curve, mastering the intricacies of AI has become a critical imperative. Buckle up, because we're about to dive into the mind bending realm of AI and uncover how it's reshaping the financial situation.

Let's start with the basics. At its core, AI is the ability of machines to mimic human intelligence, learn from data, and make decisions with minimal human intervention. From natural language processing that can decode complex financial jargon to machine learning algorithms that can identify patterns in market fluctuations, the applications of AI in fintech are as diverse as they are captivating.

One of the most exciting frontiers of AI in fintech is the realm of predictive analytics. Imagine a world where your fintech startup can anticipate client needs, market trends, and investment opportunities with uncanny precision. By using the power of AI driven data analysis, you can uncover a wealth of realizations that could give your company a decisive edge over the competition.

But the potential of AI in fintech extends far beyond mere number crunching. By integrating AI powered virtual assistants and chatbots, you can overhaul the customer experience, offering personalized guidance and support 24/7. Imagine the delight of your clients when they can have their investment questions answered in real time, without the hassle of navigating a labyrinth of phone menus or waiting in endless queues.

As you investigate deeper into the world of AI, you'll discover a universe of possibilities. Fraud detection, risk management, portfolio optimization – the list goes on. The key is to approach AI with a strategic mindset, identifying the specific is a challenge and challenges within your fintech startup and then deploying the right AI tools and technologies to address them.

AI Powered Portfolio Management

One of the most exciting applications of AI in fintech is its impact on portfolio management. Gone are the days when investment decisions were solely based on human intuition and gut feelings. AI powered portfolio management systems are revolutionizing the way wealth is managed, offering unprecedented levels of precision, efficiency, and personalization.

Imagine a scenario where your fintech startup can channel the power of machine learning algorithms to analyze vast troves of financial data, identify patterns, and make informed investment recommendations. By training these AI models on historical market data, macroeconomic trends, and individual client profiles, you can create a sophisticated, data driven investment strategy that adapts to the ever changing financial situation.

But the true magic of AI powered portfolio management lies in its ability to personalize the investment experience. Through the integration of AI driven risk assessment tools and preference matching algorithms, your fintech startup can curate customized investment portfolios tailored to each client's unique risk tolerance, financial goals, and investment timeline. Say goodbye to one size-fits all solutions and hello to a new era of personalized wealth management.

Moreover, AI powered portfolio management systems can automate the mundane tasks of portfolio rebalancing, tax loss harvesting, and asset allocation, freeing up your team to focus on delivering exceptional client service and value added perceptions. By streamlining these processes, your fintech startup can achieve greater operational efficiency, allowing you to scale your business and serve a growing client base with ease.

As you navigate the world of AI powered portfolio management, remember to strike a delicate balance between human expertise and machine intelligence. While AI can provide the analytical horsepower and decision making capabilities, the human touch of financial advisors remains vital in building trust, empathy, and long term client relationships. By seamlessly integrating these two powerful forces, your fintech startup can open up a competitive advantage that will set you apart in the ever evolving fintech scene.

Personalized Wealth Management with AI

In the world of finance, one size definitely does not fit all. Each client has unique financial goals, risk appetites, and investment preferences, and traditional wealth management approaches have often struggled to cater to these individual needs effectively. Enter the game changing realm of AI powered personalized wealth management.

Imagine a future where your fintech startup can offer a truly bespoke investment experience, tailored to the specific requirements of each and every client. Through the integration of advanced AI algorithms, your platform can investigate deep into a client's financial profile, factoring in everything from their age and income to their long term aspirations and short term cash flow needs.

Gone are the days of generic portfolio recommendations and one size-fits all financial advice. With the power of AI at your fingertips, your fintech startup can create personalized investment strategies that sync perfectly with each client's unique circumstances and goals. Imagine the delight of a young professional seeking to grow their wealth for a down payment on a dream home, or the relief of a retiree looking to preserve their hard earned assets for a comfortable retirement.

But the benefits of AI powered personalized wealth management extend far beyond mere investment optimization. By leveraging natural language processing and conversational AI, your fintech startup can offer a truly interactive and engaging client experience. Clients can communicate their financial concerns, ask for advice, and receive real time, contextual responses, all without the need for a human financial advisor.

Imagine the power of an AI driven virtual assistant that can analyze a client's financial situation, recommend tailored investment strategies, and even provide personalized financial education – all while learning and adapting to the client's preferences over time. This level of hyper personalization not only improves client satisfaction but also promotes a deeper sense of trust and loyalty, positioning your fintech startup as a trusted partner in their financial journey.

As you explore the possibilities of AI powered personalized wealth management, remember to prioritize transparency, data privacy, and ethical AI practices. By building a strong foundation of trust and accountability, your fintech startup can position itself as a beacon of innovation in an industry that is ripe for disruption.

Building a Fintech Startup with AI

Defining Your Fintech Startup's Vision

So, you've caught the fintech bug and you're ready to dive headfirst into the exhilarating world of AI powered financial services. But before you start coding up a storm or pitching to investors, take a step back and ask yourself: what's the big picture? What's the grand vision that's going to drive your startup to greatness?

It's time to don your visionary hat and let your imagination run wild. Think beyond the traditional robo advisor model and envision a future where your fintech startup is a game changer, a disruptor in the industry. Maybe it's a platform that uses AI to create truly personalized wealth management plans, or a mobile app that puts the power of predictive analytics in the palm of your customers' hands. Whatever it is, make sure it's bold, it's ambitious, and it's going to make the competition green with envy.

But don't just stop at the lofty ideas – you need to back it up with a solid strategy. Break down your vision into achievable milestones and set your sights on short term wins that will build momentum and credibility. Remember, Rome wasn't built in a day, and your fintech empire won't be either. Take it one step at a time, but always keep that grand vision in sight.

And let's not forget the all important question of "why?"

What problem are you solving, and who are you solving it for? Dive deep into the is an issue of your target market and figure out how your AI powered fintech solution can make their lives easier, more efficient, and more financially secure. Because at the end of the day, that's what's going to keep your customers coming back for more.

Identifying Key AI Capabilities

Now that you've got your vision locked in, it's time to start thinking about the nitty gritty of how you're going to make it happen. And when it comes to building a fintech startup, there's one technology that's going to be your new best friend: artificial intelligence.

But hold up, don't just start throwing AI buzzwords around and calling it a day. You need to really dig in and understand the specific AI capabilities that are going to be important for your fintech venture. Are you looking to use machine learning for predictive analytics and investment strategies? Or maybe you're eyeing natural language processing to power a smart chatbot that can provide personalized financial advice? Whatever it is, make sure you have a clear understanding of the AI tools and techniques that will be the backbone of your platform.

And don't just take our word for it – get out there and talk to the experts. Reach out to AI researchers, data scientists, and fintech innovators to pick their brains and get a better sense of the cutting edge applications of AI in the financial world. After all, you want to be at the forefront of the AI revolution, not playing catch up.

Of course, identifying the right AI capabilities is only half the battle. You'll also need to figure out how to seamlessly integrate them into your fintech platform, ensuring that the technology truly improves the user experience and delivers tangible value. This might mean building custom AI models, partnering with leading AI vendors, or even assembling a crack team of in house AI experts. Whatever route you choose, make sure it matches with your overall vision and sets your startup apart from the competition.

Developing a Sturdy AI Powered Platform

Alright, you've got your vision locked in and you've identified the key AI superpowers that are going to drive your fintech startup to success. Now it's time to get your hands dirty and start building that AI powered platform that's going to shake up the industry.

First things first, you need to make sure your data foundation is rock solid. Because without high quality, well organized financial data, your AI models are going to be about as useful as a chocolate teapot. Spend time meticulously collecting, cleaning, and structuring your data – after all, this is the fuel that's going to power your AI engine.

Once you've got that data ducks in a row, it's time to start putting your AI capabilities to work. Experiment with different machine learning algorithms and neural network architectures to find the ones that deliver the most accurate and insightful predictions. And don't be afraid to get a little creative – who knows, maybe that wacky idea you had about using reinforcement learning to fine-tune your investment strategies will be the secret sauce that sets you apart.

But building a sturdy AI powered fintech platform is about

more than just the technology – you also need to focus on the user experience. After all, what good is a cutting edge AI platform if your customers can't figure out how to use it? Invest in intuitive, user friendly interfaces that make it a breeze for your clients to access the power of your AI driven financial tools. And don't forget to continuously gather feedback and iterate on your platform to ensure it's meeting their evolving needs.

Oh, and let's not forget the all important aspect of security and compliance. As a fintech startup, you'll be handling sensitive financial data, so you need to make sure your AI powered platform is bulletproof when it comes to data privacy and regulatory requirements. Collaborate with industry experts, stay on top of the latest security standards, and never compromise on the trust and safety of your customers.

Data Driven Decision Making

Collecting and Organizing Financial Data

In the ever evolving world of fintech, the ability to use the power of data is very important. As a startup founder, you'll need to don your data wizard hat and dive headfirst into the vast ocean of financial information. But don't be intimidated - with the right approach, you can turn this daunting task into a goldmine of perceptions that will propel your AI powered platform to new heights.

First and foremost, establish a powerful data infrastructure that can seamlessly integrate and process a wide range of financial data sources. Think beyond the traditional portfolio holdings and transaction records - explore alternative data sets such as social media sentiment, news articles, and even satellite imagery. Each of these can hold the key to uncovering hidden trends and patterns that could give your startup a competitive edge.

Next, develop a meticulous data organization system that will allow you to effortlessly navigate and extract the perceptions you need. Implement a centralized data warehouse, leveraging the latest cloud based technologies to ensure scalability and accessibility. Invest in data cleansing and harmonization processes to eliminate inconsistencies and ensure the integrity of your data.

Remember, data is the lifeblood of your AI powered fintech

platform, so treat it with the care and attention it deserves. Develop a data governance framework that ensures compliance, security, and ethical usage. Enable your team to become data stewards, promoting a culture of data driven decision making that will permeate every aspect of your business.

Leveraging Machine Learning for Perceptions

Now that you've amassed a rich source of financial data, it's time to release the power of machine learning to uncover the realizations that will propel your fintech startup to new heights. Embrace the latest advancements in AI and ML, and make use of their revolutionary potential to turn your data into a competitive advantage.

Start by identifying the key questions you want to answer: How can you accurately predict market trends? Which investment strategies yield the highest returns? How can you personalize your wealth management services to better serve your clients? Armed with these guiding questions, develop a strong machine learning framework that can analyze your data, identify patterns, and generate practical realizations.

Experiment with a range of ML techniques, from supervised learning models for predicting investment performance to unsupervised algorithms for segmenting your client base. Use natural language processing to extract valuable realizations from unstructured data sources, such as news articles and social media posts. Augment your models with reinforcement learning algorithms that can continuously adapt and improve based on real world feedback.

As you examine deeper into the world of machine learning, remember to maintain a critical eye and a healthy dose of skepticism. Continuously validate your models, test their robustness, and be mindful of potential biases. Collaborate with data scientists and financial experts to ensure that your understanding are both technically sound and strategically relevant.

Predictive Analytics and Investment Strategies

With a solid data infrastructure and a suite of powerful machine learning models in place, it's time to employ the power of predictive analytics to develop inventive investment strategies that will set your fintech startup apart. Embrace the challenge of forecasting market movements, identifying undervalued assets, and crafting personalized portfolios that deliver exceptional returns.

Dive deep into the realm of time series analysis, leveraging advanced techniques like ARIMA models and neural networks to predict market fluctuations and economic indicators. Explore the potential of reinforcement learning algorithms to improve your investment strategies, constantly seeking to maximize risk adjusted returns.

But don't stop there. Incorporate alternative data sources, such as satellite imagery, social media sentiment, and web scraping, to gain a more overall understanding of market dynamics. Develop novel investment theses that capitalize on emerging trends, disruptions, and behavioral biases. Experiment with hyper personalized portfolios that cater to the unique risk profiles and investment goals of your clients.

As you navigate the complexities of predictive analytics and investment strategies, remember to maintain a healthy balance of innovation and risk management. Implement strong backtesting and stress testing frameworks to validate your models and ensure the long term sustainability of your investment approaches. Engage with industry experts, regulatory authorities, and your client base to ensure that your strategies coordinate with their needs and preferences.

Achieving Operational Efficiency with AI

Automating Mundane Tasks

In the fast paced world of fintech, time is of the essence. Fortunately, Artificial Intelligence has the power to rationalize your operations and free up your team to focus on more strategic initiatives. Say goodbye to the tedious, time consuming tasks that sap your productivity and hello to a new era of efficiency.

AI powered automation can take care of the grunt work, from data entry and client onboarding to routine portfolio rebalancing and performance reporting. By delegating these repetitive chores to intelligent algorithms, you can dramatically reduce the potential for human error and ensure a consistent, high quality output. It's like having a legion of diligent digital assistants working tirelessly behind the scenes, allowing your employees to apply their expertise where it matters most.

But the benefits of AI driven automation extend far beyond mere time savings. By automating these mundane tasks, you'll also open up the power of real time data analysis and decision making. Your AI systems can continuously monitor market conditions, client portfolios, and regulatory changes, seamlessly adjusting strategies and alerting your team to emerging opportunities or risks. This proactive, data driven approach ensures that your fintech startup remains responsive, responsive, and one step ahead of the competition.

Improving Customer Experience

In the world of fintech, the customer experience is very important. Clients today demand personalized, frictionless interactions that cater to their unique needs and preferences. Fortunately, AI is the key to uncovering a new level of customer engagement and satisfaction.

Imagine a virtual assistant that can anticipate your clients' questions, provide tailored investment advice, and seamlessly handle routine inquiries – all with the warmth and empathy of a human touch. AI powered chatbots and voice interfaces can do just that, leveraging natural language processing and machine learning to deliver a truly personalized experience. By automating the mundane aspects of customer service, your team can focus on building deeper, more meaningful relationships with your clients.

But the power of AI in improving the customer experience goes beyond just customer service. AI driven algorithms can analyze vast troves of user data to uncover realizations that inform product development, user interface design, and even marketing strategies. By truly understanding the needs, behaviors, and is a challenge of your clients, you can craft a fintech experience that anticipates their desires and exceeds their expectations – a surefire way to build brand loyalty and drive sustainable growth.

Streamlining Back Office Operations

While the front end customer experience may captivate your clients, the true heart of your fintech startup lies in its back office operations. From compliance and risk management to accounting and portfolio management, these behind the-scenes functions are the unsung heroes that keep your business running smoothly.

Fortunately, AI can work its magic here as well, revolutionizing the way you approach back office tasks. Imagine an AI powered system that can automatically detect and flag suspicious transactions, monitor for regulatory changes, and generate comprehensive financial reports – all with lightning fast speed and pinpoint accuracy. By automating these critical but often tedious processes, you can free up your team to focus on higher level strategic initiatives, while ensuring that your compliance and risk management protocols are airtight.

But the benefits of AI driven back office optimization extend even further. By integrating machine learning algorithms into your portfolio management systems, you can make accessible new levels of precision and efficiency. These AI models can continuously analyze market data, investor behavior, and portfolio performance to identify optimal asset allocation strategies, rebalance portfolios in real time, and proactively manage risk – all with an unparalleled level of sophistication and speed that would be nearly impossible for a human team to replicate.

Ensuring Regulatory Compliance

Understanding Financial Regulations

Navigating the complex web of financial regulations can feel like traversing a minefield, but it's a essential aspect of building a successful fintech startup. As you investigate into the realm of artificial intelligence and data driven decision making, it's essential to stay attuned to the ever evolving regulatory situation. Failure to comply with the diverse of rules and guidelines can not only result in hefty fines but also irreparable damage to your company's reputation.

From the moment you imagine your fintech venture, it's imperative to familiarize yourself with the regulatory bodies that oversee the financial industry in your jurisdiction. Whether it's the Financial Conduct Authority (FCA) in the United Kingdom, the Securities and Exchange Commission (SEC) in the United States, or the various regulatory frameworks across the globe, understanding the nuances of each regulatory framework is a non negotiable step in your startup's journey.

Regulations governing areas such as customer data privacy, anti money laundering (AML) protocols, and investment suitability assessments can have a deep impact on the design and implementation of your AI powered fintech solutions. Staying ahead of the curve and anticipating regulatory changes will not only help you avoid costly compliance breaches but also position your startup as a trusted and reliable partner in the eyes of your clients and industry peers.

Implementing Ethical AI Practices

As you use the power of artificial intelligence to drive your fintech startup's growth, it's vital to prioritize ethical AI practices. The integration of AI into financial services has raised concerns about bias, transparency, and accountability, and it's your responsibility as a fintech innovator to address these issues head on.

Develop a comprehensive ethical framework that guides the development and deployment of your AI powered solutions. This framework should comprise principles such as fairness, transparency, privacy, and accountability, ensuring that your AI systems treat all customers equitably and safeguard their personal information. Implement rigorous testing and auditing procedures to identify and mitigate potential sources of bias, and be proactive in communicating your ethical AI practices to both your clients and regulatory authorities.

Nurturing a culture of ethical AI within your organization is equally critical. Allow your data scientists, engineers, and product managers to advocate for ethical decision making, and provide them with the resources and training necessary to uphold the highest standards of AI governance. By embedding ethical principles into the DNA of your fintech startup, you'll not only build trust with your clients but also position your company as a responsible industry leader.

Maintaining Transparency and Accountability

As the fintech industry continues to evolve, regulators and consumers alike are demanding greater transparency and accountability from fintech companies. In an era of heightened scrutiny, it's imperative that your fintech startup adopts a proactive and transparent approach to its operations and decision making processes.

Ensure that your AI powered solutions are designed with transparency in mind, providing clear explanations of how they arrive at their recommendations and decisions. Develop powerful reporting mechanisms that allow your clients to understand the rationale behind the investment strategies and risk assessments generated by your AI systems. By encouraging a culture of transparency, you'll not only build trust with your customers but also demonstrate your commitment to responsible innovation.

Furthermore, establish well defined lines of accountability within your organization, clearly delineating the roles and responsibilities of your AI development team, compliance officers, and executive leadership. Implement powerful governance frameworks that enable you to swiftly address any issues or concerns that may arise, and be prepared to engage with regulators in a cooperative and forthcoming manner. Embracing transparency and accountability will not only safeguard your company's reputation but also contribute to the overall trustworthiness of the fintech industry.

Cybersecurity and Data Privacy

Protecting Client Information

In the high stakes world of fintech, safeguarding client data is a non negotiable imperative. It's not just about compliance – it's about preserving the trust that's the lifeblood of your business. Imagine the shockwaves if a data breach sent your clients' sensitive financial information spiraling into the dark corners of the internet. Yikes, talk about a PR nightmare that would make even the most seasoned crisis manager break out in hives.

The key is to adopt a fortress like approach to data security, one that would make even the most paranoid of tinfoil hat wearing conspiracy theorists nod in approval. Implement strong encryption protocols, multi factor authentication, and ironclad access controls. And don't forget to keep your team members on their toes with regular cybersecurity training – we're talking quizzes, simulated attacks, the whole nine yards. After all, the weakest link in any security chain is usually the human element, and you can't afford to have your employees accidentally letting the digital wolves in through the back door.

Of course, data protection isn't just about safeguarding your clients' information – it's also about preserving your own competitive edge. Trade secrets, proprietary algorithms, that brilliantly conceived marketing campaign that's sure to send your user numbers soaring – these are the crown jewels of your fintech empire, and they need to be guarded like a mother dragon hoarding her hoard of shiny gold coins.

Implementing Sturdy Security Measures

Cybersecurity is a constantly evolving battlefield, and you need to be ready to adapt and upgrade your defenses at a moment's notice. Start by conducting a comprehensive risk assessment to identify your most vulnerable points of entry. Then, layer on the security measures like there's no tomorrow – firewalls, intrusion detection systems, security information and event management (SIEM) tools, the works.

And don't forget the human element – your employees are your first line of defense against digital threats. Implement rigorous access controls, with privileges doled out on a strict need to-know basis. Encourage a culture of vigilance, where your team members are allowed to report even the slightest hint of suspicious activity. After all, who knows – that quirky looking email from the "CEO" asking for your login credentials might just be the work of a highly sophisticated phishing scam.

Of course, no security system is impenetrable, and that's why you need to have a solid incident response plan in place. When (not if) the inevitable breach occurs, you need to be ready to spring into action, containing the damage, notifying affected parties, and launching a full scale investigation to identify the vulnerabilities that allowed the attack to succeed. And don't forget to learn from your mistakes – use each incident as an opportunity to strengthen your defenses and stay one step ahead of the cybercriminals.

Addressing Emerging Cyber Threats

In the ever evolving scene of fintech, the cybersecurity challenges are as dynamic as the industry itself. Just when you think you've got your bases covered, a new threat emerges, ready to pounce on any weak spots in your digital fortress.

Take the rise of ransomware, for example – a particularly nasty breed of malware that can encrypt your critical data and hold it for ransom. It's like a digital version of the mafia, except instead of breaking your kneecaps, they're threatening to delete your company's lifeblood. And as if that weren't enough, the cybercriminals behind these attacks are constantly refining their techniques, making it a constant battle to stay one step ahead.

Then there's the growing threat of AI powered attacks, where sophisticated algorithms are used to infiltrate your systems, impersonate your employees, and wreak havoc on your operations. Imagine a scenario where a cybercriminal trains an AI model to mimic your CEO's voice and then uses it to trick your finance team into transferring funds to a rogue account. Chilling, isn't it?

To combat these emerging threats, you'll need to stay vigilant, invest in cutting edge security solutions, and develop a culture of cybersecurity awareness within your organization. Regularly update your incident response plan, conduct penetration testing to identify vulnerabilities, and stay informed about the latest industry trends and recommended approaches. Because in the high stakes world of fintech, there's no room for complacency – one slip up could be the difference between a thriving business and a spectacular implosion.

Scaling your Fintech Startup

Attracting and Retaining Talent

In the fast paced world of fintech, the secret to success lies not just in your AI powered platform, but in the brilliant minds that bring it to life. Attracting and retaining top talent is the cornerstone of scaling your startup to new heights.

Start by casting a wide net, but don't settle for just any resume that lands in your inbox. Look for individuals who possess a unique blend of technical expertise, entrepreneurial spirit, and a deep understanding of the financial industry. These are the unicorns who can navigate the complexities of fintech and transform your vision into reality.

Offer competitive salaries, of course, but don't stop there. Sweeten the deal with perks that speak to the hearts and minds of your potential hires. Think outside the box – a fully stocked kombucha bar, unlimited vacation days, or even a chance to name the company's first AI assistant. Remember, you're not just selling a job, but a lifestyle that matches with the values of your target candidates.

But the real magic happens when you nurture a culture of innovation and collaboration. Encourage your team to experiment, take risks, and shake up the status quo. Host hackathons, offer mentorship programs, and create a safe space for bold ideas to flourish. This not only attracts the best and brightest, but it also keeps them engaged and motivated to push the boundaries of what's possible.

And never underestimate the power of recognition. Celebrate your team's victories, big and small, and enable them to be the heroes of their own stories. When your employees feel valued and appreciated, they'll be more inclined to stay on board and help you navigate the ever evolving fintech scene.

Encouraging a Culture of Innovation

In the fast paced world of fintech, innovation is the lifeblood that keeps your startup alive and thriving. But nurturing a culture of innovation is no easy feat – it requires a delicate balance of vision, creativity, and a willingness to embrace the unexpected.

Start by infusing your company's DNA with a constant curiosity. Encourage your team to constantly question the status quo, explore unconventional solutions, and experiment with emerging technologies. Embrace a "fail fast, learn faster" mindset, where setbacks are seen as opportunities to refine and improve.

Next, break down the silos that can stifle innovation. Bring together cross functional teams, mix and match skillsets, and let the sparks fly. You never know when the brilliant mind of a data scientist and the out of-the box thinking of a marketing guru will collide to create the next big fintech breakthrough.

But innovation is more than just a buzzword – it's a living, breathing entity that needs to be nurtured and celebrated. Allocate dedicated resources for R&D, from hackathons to innovation labs. Equip your team to take calculated risks and provide the support they need to turn their bold ideas into reality.

Remember, true innovation doesn't happen in a vacuum. Seek out partnerships with industry leaders, academic institutions, and even your competitors. Collaborate, share knowledge, and challenge each other to push the boundaries of what's possible. After all, a rising tide lifts all boats – and in the world of fintech, that tide is powered by a shared commitment to innovation.

Expanding into New Markets

As your fintech startup gains momentum, the temptation to expand into new markets can be irresistible. But taking the leap into unfamiliar territory requires a strategic, well planned approach that balances ambition with pragmatism.

First, conduct a thorough market analysis to identify the most promising opportunities. Look for regions with a thriving financial sector, a growing middle class, and a regulatory setting that's friendly to fintech innovators. Don't just follow the herd – dig deeper to uncover hidden gems that your competitors may have overlooked.

Once you've identified your target markets, it's time to customize your selections to meet the unique needs and preferences of these new audiences. This might involve adapting your AI powered platform to accommodate different languages, currencies, or financial regulations. It could also mean developing entirely new products or services tailored to the local market.

But expansion isn't just about expanding your product line – it's also about building a strong local presence. Establish strategic partnerships with regional banks, fintech accelerators, or influential industry players who can help you navigate the local terrain and gain the trust of potential clients. And don't forget to invest in localized marketing and branding efforts to connect with your new audience in a meaningful way.

As you venture into uncharted territory, be prepared to be nimble and adaptable. Monitor your performance closely, solicit feedback from your new customers, and be ready to adjust your strategy as needed. The fintech scene is ever evolving, and the ability to respond quickly to changing market dynamics will be the key to your success.

Remember, scaling your fintech startup isn't just about numbers and metrics – it's about encouraging a culture of innovation, attracting the best and brightest talent, and staying nimble in the face of constant change. With the right mindset and the right team, the opportunities for growth are endless.

Navigating the Fintech Community

Collaborating with Traditional Financial Institutions

In the fast paced world of fintech, one thing is clear: collaboration is the name of the game. While the allure of shaking up the industry might be tempting, the savviest fintech startups know that forging strategic partnerships with traditional financial institutions can be the key to opening up exponential growth.

Sure, you could go the lone wolf route, but trust me, it's a lonely and uphill battle. These legacy institutions have resources, expertise, and established client bases that can catapult your fintech startup to new heights. Think of it like riding a rocket powered unicorn - you'll cover way more ground than trying to pedal a tricycle through a minefield.

So, how do you navigate these uncharted waters? First, ditch the 'us vs. them' mentality. These institutions aren't your enemies; they're potential allies. Approach them with an open mind, and focus on finding ways to complement their strengths and address their is a challenge. Maybe you've got the slick user interface they've been dreaming of, or perhaps your AI driven realizations can help them make better investment decisions.

But here's the kicker: it's not just about what you can offer them. You've also got to be willing to learn from their experience and adapt your approach accordingly. After all, these institutions have weathered countless storms and know the industry inside out. Tap into that knowledge, and you might just find the secret sauce to propelling your fintech startup to new levels of success.

Leveraging Fintech Partnerships

Ah, the world of fintech partnerships – it's like a high stakes game of chess, but with fewer knights and more algorithms. While collaborating with traditional financial institutions can be a game changer, don't forget the power of forging strategic alliances with other fintech players. These partnerships can reveal a whole new world of opportunities, from cross pollinating customer bases to sharing cutting edge technology.

Think about it this way: your fintech startup might have the world's most incredible wealth management platform, but if you're only reaching a small pool of clients, you're missing out on a world of potential. By partnering with a complementary fintech firm that specializes in, say, digital lending, you suddenly have access to a whole new audience – and they, in turn, get to make use of your top notch portfolio management tools.

But it's not just about customer acquisition. These partnerships can also be a wellspring of innovation. Imagine the possibilities when you combine your AI powered investment strategies with a partner's blockchain based authentication system. The result? A smooth, secure, and hyper personalized experience that leaves your competitors scratching their heads.

Of course, finding the right fintech partners is no easy feat. You've got to do your due diligence, ensure cultural alignment, and negotiate terms that benefit both parties. But trust me, the payoff is worth it. Just think of the chaos you can release when you assemble a Voltron esque squad of fintech superstars. The industry will never know what hit them.

Staying Ahead of Industry Trends

In the fast paced world of fintech, if you're not constantly scanning the horizon for the next big thing, you might as well pack up your desk and start looking for a new career. The industry moves at the speed of light, and the only way to stay ahead of the curve is to be a unceasing student of the game.

Sure, you can rely on those industry reports and market analysis, but let's be real – by the time they hit your inbox, they're already out of date. No, to truly stay ahead of the curve, you've got to get your hands dirty. Immerse yourself in the fintech community, attend every conference and meetup you can, and strike up conversations with the movers and shakers.

And let's not forget the power of social media. Follow the is a trendsetter, the disruptors, and the risk takers. Heck, start your own LinkedIn group and watch the ideas flow like a never ending stream of digital cash. You never know what unexpected realizations might spark the next big breakthrough for your fintech startup.

But it's not just about staying informed – you've got to be

willing to experiment, too. Don't be afraid to dip your toes into the latest financial technologies, even if they might seem a bit far fetched at first. Who knows, that blockchain based micro investing platform might just be the key to opening up a whole new revenue stream. The key is to stay curious, stay nimble, and be prepared to adapt at a moment's notice. Because in the world of fintech, the only constant is change.

Marketing and Branding in the Fintech Space

Crafting a Compelling Brand Identity

In the ever evolving fintech situation, your brand identity is the heartbeat that sets you apart from the competition. Forget about those cookie cutter, corporate looking logos - it's time to channel your inner creative genius and free a brand that'll have everyone talking. Think bold, think daring, think "I can't believe they actually did that!"

Forget about playing it safe, my friend. Here's a wild idea: what if your fintech startup had a mascot that was a sassy, talking piggy bank? Or maybe you could embrace the power of puns and name your robo advisor "Algorhythm." The key is to create a brand that's so unforgettable, it'll stick in people's minds like chewing gum on the bottom of their favorite shoes.

But don't just take my word for it. Look at the trailblazers who've already carved out their own path. Robinhood, for instance, managed to make investing feel like a game, complete with a cheeky logo that looks like it was designed by a caffeine fueled graphic designer on a sugar high. And let's not forget about Acorns, the fintech app that's making saving and investing as easy as, well, collecting acorns.

So, what's the secret sauce? It's all about finding that perfect balance between professionalism and personality. Your brand should scream "we know what we're doing, but we're also not afraid to have a little fun." After all, who says finance has to be synonymous with stuffy and boring? Break the mold, my friends, and let your brand's true colors shine through.

Effective Digital Marketing Strategies

Alright, folks, it's time to talk about the real magic - digital marketing. Forget those old school tactics like billboards and direct mail (unless you're feeling particularly nostalgic for the 1990s). In the fast paced world of fintech, you need to be where your target audience is: online and on their smartphones.

First things first, let's address the elephant in the room: social media. It's no longer just a place to share cat videos and argue about politics - it's a powerful tool for connecting with your customers. But don't just post the same boring updates about your latest product features. Get creative, get quirky, get downright weird. Remember that time the Wendy's Twitter account roasted someone for liking their burger a little too rare? That's the kind of energy you want to channel.

And let's not forget about content marketing. Instead of bombarding your audience with endless sales pitches, why not position yourself as a expert in the fintech space? Write blog posts that tackle the industry's biggest challenges, create informative videos that break down complex financial concepts, or host webinars that leave your audience feeling enlightened and inspired. After all, the more value you provide, the more they'll be drawn to your brand like a moth to a shiny, digital flame.

But wait, there's more! Email marketing is still alive and kicking, my friends. Craft newsletters that are so captivating, your subscribers will actually look forward to opening them. Throw in a few irresistible offers, a dash of humor, and a sprinkle of personal touch, and you've got a recipe for digital marketing gold.

Building a Powerful Client Acquisition Pipeline

Alright, let's talk about the lifeblood of your fintech startup: clients. You can have the most original technology, the most brilliant team, and the most eye catching branding, but if you can't attract and retain a steady stream of loyal customers, well, let's just say your startup is about as useful as a chocolate teapot.

So, how do you build a client acquisition pipeline that's as reliable as a Swiss watch? First and foremost, it's all about building relationships. Forget those impersonal, mass emailed pitch decks - get out there and network, network, network. Attend industry events, connect with potential partners on LinkedIn, and don't be afraid to get a little creative (have you considered hosting a fintech themed karaoke night? Just saying).

But let's not forget about the digital realm. You've already mastered the art of digital marketing, so now it's time to put those skills to work. Fine-tune your website for search engines, create irresistible lead magnets that capture your audience's attention, and make use of the power of targeted advertising to reach your ideal clients. And let's not forget about good old fashioned referrals - encourage your satisfied customers to spread the word about your fintech wizardry.

Remember, client acquisition is a delicate dance, and you've got to be willing to step out of your comfort zone and try new things. Maybe that means sponsoring a local sports team, or perhaps it's time to embrace the power of influencer marketing (just make sure you steer clear of those shady "fintech gurus" with more Instagram followers than brain cells).

The key is to never stop experimenting, never stop innovating, and never stop thinking outside the box. Because in the fast paced world of fintech, the only thing that's predictable is change - and the companies that embrace that change, well, they're the ones that'll be laughing all the way to the proverbial bank.

Securing Funding and Investments

Exploring Funding Options

Ah, the eternal conundrum of every fintech startup – how do we get our hands on that sweet, sweet cash? Well, folks, buckle up because we're about to take a wild ride through the world of funding options. From the traditional VC route to the more unconventional crowdfunding paths, we'll leave no stone unturned in our quest for financial dominance.

First off, let's talk venture capital. These are the big money players, the ones with their fingers in every fintech pie. But let me tell you, getting their attention is like trying to catch a greased up wombat in a lightning storm. It's not for the faint of heart, my friends. You better have your pitch deck polished to perfection, your numbers crunched with the precision of a Swiss watchmaker, and your charisma turned up to 11. If you can pull it off, though, the rewards can be nothing short of life changing.

Now, if you're feeling a little more adventurous, why not explore the world of crowdfunding? Imagine tapping into the collective power of the masses, each person chipping in a few bucks to help bring your fintech dreams to life. It's like a financial flash mob, but with way fewer dance moves. The key here is to get creative, to come up with a campaign that's so irresistible, people will be lining up to throw their hard earned cash at you. Think outside the box, my friends – maybe offer exclusive access to your AI powered investment strategies or a chance to be the first to beta test your robo advisor app.

And let's not forget about good old fashioned bootstrapping. Sure, it might take a little longer to get off the ground, but there's something to be said for the satisfaction of building your fintech empire one penny at a time. Pinch those pennies, scrimp and save, and before you know it, you'll have enough to get the ball rolling. Just don't forget to treat yourself to the occasional avocado toast – you need to keep that creative spark alive, after all.

Pitching to Investors

Alright, you've figured out your funding options – now it's time to put on your best show-and-tell performance and wow those deep pocketed investors. This is where the real magic happens, folks, so get ready to channel your inner Barnum & Bailey.

First and foremost, know your audience. These aren't your run of-the mill venture capitalists – they're a detecting bunch, the kind who can smell a weak pitch from a mile away. So, do your homework, understand their investment philosophies, and tailor your presentation accordingly. Are they all about that sweet, sweet ROI? Accentuate your cutting edge algorithms and projected returns. Or maybe they're more interested in addressing social issues? Highlight your fintech's potential to authorize the underbanked and promote financial inclusion.

And let's not forget the all important visuals. Your slides better be slicker than a freshly oiled otter, with infographics that would make even the most seasoned data analyst swoon. But don't just rely on the numbers – sprinkle in a few personal anecdotes, a dash of humor, and a generous helping of passion. After all, these investors aren't just looking for a good investment, they're looking for a team they can get excited about.

Lastly, be ready to answer the tough questions. These folks didn't get to where they are by being easily impressed, so be prepared to dive deep into the nitty gritty of your business model, your go to-market strategy, and your plans for world domination. And for the love of all things fintech, don't try to BS your way through – honesty and transparency are the name of the game here.

Managing Investor Relations

Alright, you've managed to convince those deep pocketed investors to take a chance on your fintech dream – now the real work begins. Because let me tell you, maintaining those relationships is like trying to herd a bunch of cats through a laser light show.

First and foremost, communication is key. These investors aren't just looking for a return on their investment; they want to feel like they're a part of the journey. So, make sure you're keeping them in the loop, sharing updates (both the good and the bad), and being transparent about your successes and challenges. And for the love of all things holy, don't ghost them – that's a surefire way to end up on the investor blacklist faster than you can say "algorithmic trading."

Speaking of challenges, be prepared to navigate a minefield of differing opinions and agendas. Remember, these investors aren't just writing checks – they're bringing their own experiences, biases, and egos to the table. It's your job to find a way to balance their input with your own vision, all while maintaining a sense of harmony and trust. It's a delicate dance, to be sure, but trust me, the payoff is worth it.

And let's not forget the good old fashioned art of networking. These investors aren't just your funders, they're your connections to a whole new world of opportunity. Use those relationships, make introductions, and see where they can help you take your fintech startup to the next level. After all, it's not just about the money – it's about building a powerful network that can weather any storm.

So, there you have it, folks – the keys to securing funding and managing those all important investor relations. It's a wild ride, to be sure, but if you can navigate the ups and downs, the twists and turns, you just might find yourself sitting on a fintech empire bigger than your wildest dreams. Now go forth, my friends, and let the funding frenzy begin!

Adapting to a Changing Regulatory Setting

Monitoring Regulatory Updates

In the fast paced world of fintech, staying ahead of the regulatory curve is a never ending challenge. As your AI powered startup navigates the ever evolving setting, it's essential to maintain a vigilant eye on the latest developments. After all, one wrong step could send you tumbling down a rabbit hole of legal complications faster than you can say "algorithmic trading."

But fear not, my fellow fintech pioneers! Embrace the chaos, for it is the gateway to innovation. Designate a team of regulatory ninjas, equipped with lightning fast reflexes and a thirst for knowledge that would make even the most seasoned bureaucrat quiver in their boots. These intrepid souls will scour the depths of government websites, attend industry conferences, and network with the sharpest legal minds to keep your startup one step ahead of the game.

Develop relationships with regulatory bodies, lawmakers, and industry associations. Attend town halls, write op eds, and make your voice heard. Become the fintech influencer that everyone is clamoring to consult. After all, who better to shape the future of the industry than the ones who are blazing the trail?

Ensuring Compliance with New Rules

Navigating the ever evolving regulatory situation is like a high stakes game of chess, where a single misstep can cost you dearly. But fear not, for your fintech startup is armed with the ultimate weapon: a crack team of compliance experts who can dance through the minefield of rules and regulations like Fred Astaire on a tightrope.

Invest in a powerful compliance management system that can keep track of the many of requirements, from Know Your Customer (KYC) protocols to anti money laundering (AML) regulations. Automate the monotonous tasks, freeing up your team to focus on the strategic aspects of compliance. And when the regulators come knocking (and they will, oh, they will), greet them with a smile and a playbook that would make a military strategist weep with joy.

But compliance is not just about ticking boxes and appeasing the powers that be. It's about nurturing a culture of integrity and accountability within your organization. Authorize your employees to be vigilant watchdogs, authorized to identify and report potential issues before they become full blown disasters. After all, a single slip up can figure out the very fabric of your fintech empire.

Advocating for Fintech Friendly Policies

In the ever evolving world of fintech, the only constant is change. And with change comes the need to advocate for policies that nurture innovation and protect the rights of both startups and consumers. It's a delicate dance, where you must navigate the treacherous waters of bureaucracy while maintaining a steady beat of progress.

Assemble a crack team of policy experts, armed with the latest data, research, and a keen understanding of the political terrain. These policy ninjas will become your voice in the corridors of power, lobbying for regulations that promote a thriving fintech community. Whether it's pushing for sandboxes that allow for controlled experimentation or advocating for data privacy laws that safeguard client information, your team will be the vanguard, leading the charge for a future where fintech and regulation coexist in perfect harmony.

But don't just leave it to the professionals. Allow your entire organization to become ambassadors for the fintech cause. Encourage employees to engage with policymakers, attend industry events, and share their understanding and experiences. After all, the true power of advocacy lies in the collective voice of those who have seen the radical potential of fintech firsthand.

Encouraging Client Trust and Loyalty

Prioritizing Transparency and Communication

In the fast paced and ever evolving world of fintech, where innovation is the name of the game, it's all too easy to get caught up in the glitz and glamour of the latest technological breakthroughs. But let's not forget the most important ingredient in the recipe for success: trust. Building and maintaining trust with your clients should be the bedrock of your fintech startup's operations.

Transparency is the key that reveals the door to trust. Your clients deserve to know exactly what they're getting, how it works, and why it's the best solution for their financial needs. No more smoke and mirrors, my friend - it's time to pull back the curtain and let your clients see the inner workings of your AI powered magic.

Start by being upfront about your fees, your investment strategies, and the potential risks involved. Sure, it might not be the sexiest topic, but it's essential for building long lasting relationships with your clients. And when it comes to communicating this information, don't just rely on dense legal jargon or technical mumbo jumbo. Craft your messaging with a human touch, using clear and accessible language that your clients can actually understand.

But transparency doesn't stop there. Keep your clients in the loop every step of the way, whether it's through regular updates, personalized portfolio reviews, or open door Q&A sessions. Remember, your clients aren't just numbers in a spreadsheet – they're individuals with unique goals, concerns, and expectations. By nurturing open and honest communication, you'll not only build trust, but you'll also gain indispensable realizations that can help you refine your services and stay one step ahead of the competition.

Providing Exceptional Customer Service

In the world of fintech, where the competition is fierce and the setting is constantly evolving, providing exceptional customer service can be the difference between a loyal client and a disgruntled one. And let's be real, when it comes to their hard earned money, your clients are going to have high expectations – and rightfully so.

But here's the thing: exceptional customer service isn't just about answering phone calls and responding to emails within a nanosecond (although those things certainly help). It's about going above and beyond, anticipating your clients' needs, and delivering a level of personalized attention that leaves them feeling like they're the most important person in the room.

Think about it this way: your clients are entrusting you with their financial well being, which is a pretty big deal. So, how can you make them feel valued, heard, and supported every step of the way? Maybe it's sending a handwritten thank you note after a particularly challenging transaction, or offering to connect them with a financial planner to discuss their long term goals. Or perhaps it's simply taking the time to explain a complex concept in a way that makes them feel allowed and informed.

And let's not forget the power of technology. By leveraging the AI powered tools at your disposal, you can make efficient administrative tasks, automate personalized communications, and free up your team to focus on delivering an exceptional customer experience. Just remember to strike the right balance – you don't want your clients to feel like they're interacting with a robot, after all.

Cultivating Long Term Relationships

In the cutthroat world of fintech, it's easy to get caught up in the constant pursuit of new clients. But let's not forget the true gold mine that lies within your existing client base. By cultivating long term relationships, you'll not only secure a steady stream of revenue, but you'll also build a loyal following that can serve as a powerful marketing tool for your fintech startup.

The key to nurturing these long term relationships? Treat your clients like the valuable partners they are. Engage with them on a personal level, show genuine interest in their lives and their financial goals, and make them feel like they're more than just a number on a spreadsheet.

And let's not forget the power of surprises and delights. Whether it's a handwritten birthday card, a personalized gift, or an invitation to an exclusive event, these little touches can go a long way in making your clients feel appreciated and valued. After all, who doesn't love a bit of unexpected joy in their inbox or mailbox?

Of course, cultivating long term relationships isn't just about the warm and fuzzy stuff. It's also about continuously evolving your services to meet your clients' changing needs. Stay on top of industry trends, listen to their feedback, and be nimble enough to adapt your services accordingly. By demonstrating your commitment to their financial well being, you'll not only retain your clients but also turn them into raving advocates for your fintech startup.

Leveraging Emerging Technologies

Exploring Blockchain and Cryptocurrencies

Hold onto your wallets, folks, because we're about to dive into the wild world of blockchain and cryptocurrencies. These cutting edge technologies are poised to unsettle the traditional financial situation, and your fintech startup can't afford to be left behind.

Let's start by addressing the elephant in the room: Bitcoin. Sure, it's had its fair share of wild price swings and dubious associations, but don't let that overshadow the revolutionary potential of the underlying blockchain technology. This distributed, decentralized ledger has the power to rationalize countless financial processes, from cross border payments to secure data storage.

But Bitcoin is just the tip of the cryptocurrency iceberg. Ethereum, Ripple, Litecoin, and a host of other digital currencies are vying for their slice of the fintech pie. Each offers unique features and use cases, and it's up to you to explore which ones might be the best fit for your fintech startup's needs. Perhaps a cryptocurrency powered remittance service could be your next big innovation? Or maybe a blockchain based peer to-peer lending platform is more your speed?

Just remember, as you wade into the crypto waters, it's critical to stay on top of the ever evolving regulatory terrain.

Work closely with legal experts to ensure your blockchain powered products and services are compliant with the latest rules and regulations. And be prepared to navigate the complex world of cryptocurrency wallets, exchanges, and storage solutions – your clients will be counting on you to keep their digital assets safe and secure.

Integrating Voice Assistants and Chatbots

In the blink of an eye, voice assistants and chatbots have gone from sci fi fantasies to omnipresent features in our everyday lives. And in the world of fintech, these AI powered tools are poised to transform the way we interact with our money.

Imagine a world where your clients can simply ask Alexa to check their account balances, or have a friendly chatbot guide them through the process of opening a new investment portfolio. These conversational interfaces aren't just a gimmick – they can dramatically improve the customer experience, simplify administrative tasks, and even provide personalized financial advice.

But integrating voice assistants and chatbots into your fintech startup's system isn't as simple as just plugging in a plug and-play solution. You'll need to carefully consider the user experience, data privacy concerns, and the overall integration with your existing AI powered platform. Will your chatbot be a witty, sarcastic problem solver, or a warm, empathetic financial confidant? The choice is yours, but it can make all the difference in how your clients perceive and interact with your brand.

And don't forget, as you explore into the world of conversational AI, you'll need to stay on top of the rapidly evolving technology scene. Keep a close eye on the latest advancements in natural language processing, sentiment analysis, and machine learning – these capabilities will be the key to building voice assistants and chatbots that truly understand and meet the needs of your fintech clients.

Utilizing the Power of the Internet of Things

In the not so-distant future, your fintech startup's services won't just be confined to smartphones and laptops. No, the real magic is going to happen when your AI powered financial tools start seamlessly integrating with the growing network of connected devices that make up the Internet of Things (IoT).

Imagine a world where your client's smart refrigerator can automatically trigger a transfer to their savings account every time they order a pizza. Or a scenario where their fitness tracker can provide real time observations into their spending habits, helping them make more informed financial decisions. The possibilities are endless, and the implications for the future of fintech are downright mind boggling.

Of course, using the power of the IoT isn't as simple as just slapping a few sensors on a toaster and calling it a day. You'll need to navigate the complex web of device protocols, data integration, and cybersecurity concerns. But get it right, and you can open up a goldmine of valuable user data that can power everything from personalized investment strategies to predictive fraud detection.

And let's not forget about the sheer coolness factor. Imagine a world where your fintech startup's services are seamlessly woven into the fabric of your clients' everyday lives, making financial management as easy and intuitive as turning on the lights or adjusting the thermostat. It's the kind of futuristic, sci fi-inspired innovation that can help your brand stand out in the crowded fintech setting.

The Future of Fintech and AI

Anticipating Industry Disruptions

Hold onto your robo hats, my friends, because the future of fintech is about to get wild. We're talking disruptions that'll make the advent of the internet look like a mere ripple in the digital ocean. And at the heart of it all? Artificial intelligence, that ever evolving chameleon of technology.

Picture this: your trusty robo advisor, once a beacon of predictable portfolio management, will morph into a true financial sorcerer. With the power of AI, it'll be able to anticipate market shifts like a psychic with a crystal ball, leaving your poor human money managers in the dust, frantically trying to catch up.

But that's just the beginning. Imagine a world where your digital assistant doesn't just manage your finances, but actually becomes your financial confidant, offering personalized advice that's so spot on, it's as if it's peering directly into the depths of your soul. No more cookie cutter solutions, my friends – it'll be a symphony of tailored financial symphonies, orchestrated by the virtuosos of artificial intelligence.

And hold onto your wallets, because the blockchain revolution is about to take the fintech world by storm. Imagine a future where your transactions are faster than a bolt of lightning, and your data is locked tighter than Fort

Knox. Goodbye, paperwork; hello, digital empires built on the foundations of cryptocurrency and distributed ledger technology.

But the real game changer? The fusion of AI and blockchain. Picture a world where your financial decisions are made with the prescience of a Jedi Master, and your transactions are executed with the speed and security of a high tech fortress. It's a future where the line between finance and science fiction blurs, and the only limit is your imagination.

Preparing for Technological Advancements

As the fintech scene evolves, one thing is certain: the pace of technological change will only accelerate. And for those who want to stay ahead of the curve, the key is to embrace the unknown and be ready to adapt at a moment's notice.

Let's start with the elephant in the room: quantum computing. While it may sound like something straight out of a sci fi novel, the reality is that this revolutionary technology is poised to shake up the world of finance like never before. Imagine algorithms that can crack even the most secure encryption protocols, making traditional cybersecurity measures obsolete. It's a game changer that will force fintech startups to rethink their entire approach to data protection and privacy.

But the quantum conundrum is just the tip of the iceberg. In the years to come, we'll see the rise of advanced natural language processing, enabling AI assistants to engage in continuous, human like conversations with clients. Imagine a future where your robo advisor not only manages your portfolio, but also serves as your personal financial confidant, offering realizations and advice that are indistinguishable from those of a flesh and-blood wealth manager.

And let's not forget the potential of edge computing, where data processing and decision making happen right at the edge of the network, rather than in a centralized cloud. This could change radically the way fintech startups handle sensitive financial data, reducing latency and increasing security in ways we've only dreamed of.

The bottom line? Fintech entrepreneurs who want to stay ahead of the curve need to keep a constant eye on the horizon, anticipating the next wave of technological breakthroughs and positioning their companies to ride the crest of innovation. Because in the fast paced world of fintech, those who fail to adapt will quickly find themselves left behind, while the true visionaries will reap the rewards of their foresight.

Envisioning the Next Generation of Fintech

As we gaze into the crystal ball of fintech's future, one thing is clear: the industry is about to undergo a intense transformation that will redefine the way we think about money, investment, and personal finance.

Imagine a world where your digital assistant doesn't just manage your portfolio, but actively collaborates with you to craft a financial strategy that's tailored to your unique needs and aspirations. Gone will be the days of one size-fits all solutions, replaced by a comprehensive, AI powered approach that takes into account your life goals, risk tolerance, and even your emotional relationship with money.

And what about the role of the traditional financial advisor? In the brave new world of fintech, these seasoned professionals will evolve into something akin to financial sherpa, guiding their clients through the increasingly complex situation of investment options, tax implications, and regulatory changes. But with the power of AI at their fingertips, they'll be able to offer a level of personalized service that was once unimaginable.

But the real game changer? The integration of blockchain technology with AI driven wealth management. Imagine a future where your financial transactions are executed with the speed and security of a high tech fortress, while your investment decisions are made with the prescience of a Jedi Master. It's a world where the line between finance and science fiction blurs, and the only limit is your imagination.

And let's not forget the potential impact of emerging technologies like quantum computing and edge computing. As these game changers enter the fintech arena, we'll see a radical shift in the way data is processed, secured, and leveraged to drive unprecedented levels of personalization and efficiency.

So, what does the future of fintech hold? In a word: boundless. As AI, blockchain, and other cutting edge technologies converge, we're on the precipice of a financial revolution that will redefine the way we think about money, investment, and personal finance. For those brave enough to embrace the unknown, the rewards will be vast – but the risks will be equally significant. Are you ready to take the leap?

Silas Meadowlark

www.ingramcontent.com/pod-product-compliance
Lightning Source LLC
Chambersburg PA
CBHW030503220526
45464CB00006B/2642